MW01124072

TEARS

THE SERIES

PSYCHOLOGICAL
WARFARE

PERCY FAIRLEY JR

WRITERS REPUBLIC L.L.C.
515 Summit Ave. Unit R1
Union City, NJ 07087, USA

Website: *www.writersrepublic.com*
Hotline: *1-877-656-6838*
Email: *info@writersrepublic.com*

Ordering Information:
Quantity sales. Special discounts are available on quantity purchases by corporations, associations, and others. For details, contact the publisher at the address above.

Library of Congress Control Number: 2023933133
ISBN-13:   979-8-88536-406-5   [Paperback Edition]
                  979-8-88810-702-7   [Hardback Edition]
                  979-8-88536-407-2   [Digital Edition]

Rev. date: 02/17/2023

I'd like to thank Writers Republic for giving me this opportunity to express my thoughts, feelings, and beliefs in a widespread format in order to reach as many people as I can. I'd like to thank my parents for the becoming of who I am and my whole family for being the support system anyone could desire. My amazing, wonderful, beautiful, the best girlfriend anyone could ask for Ashley Cade, I love you. All my friends who read and critiqued my writings and helped me believe I could make this happen and take this leap in the right direction. I love you all and Tears: The Series will not stop here.

Jambo! My name is Percy Lee Fairley and I've always had an affinity with helping other people express how they feel and to be that person there for them when they need it. I can't understand or relate to everyone in the world but that's why I decided to write a book; I'd like to help as many people around the world see that they aren't alone and it will be okay. That I promise you. I hope you enjoy all of my writings or even one of them and that maybe something resonates with you. Thank you so so so much.

(Jambo is hello/hi in swahili as a less formal greeting for example, a friend or family member.)

INHALE

EXHALE

Together

Through the drought of my empty brainstorms and after I've wrung all of the empty promises out of my heart, deep down in my soul lies a demon you've come to quell.

Took your heart full of hope and wonder just to fill mine halfway to make us equal, two storms too powerful that no one could split our sky in two, for we are together.

The rain from our blood, sweat, and tears nourishes our new found land and seedlings yet to grow. Two pairs of eyes for a pair of I's that make a we are forever conjoined in a life meant to be.

Anguish

My mind state has a city called doubt in which you reside to fish at the lake of despair using my optimism as bait. Envious of my success you tear and claw at my spirits but you forgot it's a ghost town. A town that I created because you're dead to me. The you that I knew never to be known again.

My mind has a city called memory but I miss you and it's destroying me, as you invade my dreams, my hope dwindles as I ponder about what we had. A crescent moon how you never show the real you only fragments of who you want to be.

Pacifist

I can't see the light behind these fights because rather than light they are in spite of darkness. Hoping to fill the world with pollution because according to darkness there is no solution, But light has a plan to ban the darkness before it ever crosses the sands of our lands

Lash Out

Under siege was my heart, suffocating from the deafening march by your soldiers of love and I received you with gates ajar. As you pierce, hack, and slash at my heart I draw you in closer, making you cut deeper though I endure the pain for you are my love.

Starving for your affection so much so that when you come around it's like a rush, love I can't have enough. Distraught when you leave yet, conflicted on why you come back and I still reach for you. The epitome of a rose how you've grown on me making it impossible to see through your beautiful foliage.

Human

Change can come from a vast range starting from climate change to verbal confrontation. Increasing the inflation of inflammation in a raging nation causing more deforestation. Depression, oppression, and aggression all grow from the roots of deforestation.

These roots can't simply be ripped out, they go deep starting as fluorescent trees who get cut down and shaped to their farmers' vision which I've found unsound.

It takes just as many to pause as it does to cause this should be anomaly but cause we shall not because it's already caused a lot. Starting from pain to su ering, blame to murdering, not even considering that change is reckoning.

O

Intrepid souls yearning for what could be, Insecurities masking your tracks. Misdirection further straying us down different paths, which one will you take? The yellow brick road chasing a fantasy?

???

A compression on my chest, gasping for air, what is this weight I'm carrying? Plenty of fish in the sea, does that include the predators? What if I'm devoured searching for you? The tide and currents misguide me, cast me further down a mysterious path.

Do I follow? Do I fight? Where will it lead me? Plenty of fish in the sea but what if you're not a fish at all? What if you're a mammal or a bird, how will I reach you? They say never change for anyone and always be yourself but I'd alter my genomes to be with you, is that healthy?

Plenty of fish in the sea but what about all the fish that follow the same philosophy and believe that I'm the fish for them? How do I reject them because aren't you? What if I'm the reason they lose all hope?

My mind is racing and I can't breathe, why can't I steady my breath? I haven't eaten, I forgot about my own health stressing if you exist, stressing what is existence? Don't want it if it doesn't involve you so I live my whole life searching for you, you? Where am I? Who am I? Is that you?

Plenty of fish in the sea so how do I know we'll meet? What if I die alone looking for you? What if you're the one for me but I'm not the one for you? What if in finding you, I lose myself?

I Cry When I Shower

When it rains it pours, drizzles down my face but I'm faceless, no time to face it. Cries for help obscured by anonymity. Am I unseen or ignored? An open book with no chapters you can read me but do you understand? I bleed on every page but I only have so much blood to give until I'm drained so I cry in the shower to disguise my tears, no one notices my despair anyway.

Vulnerable

To open up isn't to be weak. Allowing yourself the luxury of releasing everything pent up inside makes room for your blossom to expand, what a beautiful foliage. Roses, tulips, and lavender; all uniquely different yet still in their own way the same. Expand into something more copious and let everyone know what makes you uniquely you.

Pastel Hearts

Pastel Hearts devoid of reality how my hypocrisy reflects your true motive. Are you scared of us because of your true colors? How they lack primary priorities and leave me secondary, irrelevant.

Terrified of how perfect we were, a dubious reality tormented by overthinking. Controlled by the laws of my mental state remarking "what if" clashing perspectives cause me to concede within the confines of my heart. The vibrant hues fading.

Soothsayer

You manipulate and recycle my feelings and emotions, the power you have over me is nonsensical. Aura like quicksand every grain representing your recurrent lies and false promises, unapproachable.

Conscious of my kind soul you befoul it when I open up. Unable to mask it because you broke the hinges off of my vessel but who am I without you?

Conscious

Among the paths most slighted is where your fate is decided. The long and arduous venture strives to strife your determination and tear you down. Drag your tattered clothes through the mud and don't let the void of your consciousness subdue you. As you tread through the barren lands you see those who have fallen to the perils of their own mind stuck in the mud as their brains storm; but you have a solid ground, a foundation to lean on, so protect it. Protecting it by never giving up as giving up means breaking the foundation yourself and everything you've worked for. By keeping true to the promise you chose to let burden you, no affliction can bare itself upon thee.

Statistics

Mountain man, why must you work so hard? For every mountain you move they give you a pebble in return yet you still work so hard. "Well valley, with all the pebbles I'm rewarded I hope to build my own mountain one day." So you want to build your mountain by using pieces of others? What happens when their mountains fall and collapse? Will you pick off their scraps as well? "Of course I will! It's the way of life, take or be taken from." What about me? I'm a valley far far below the mountains and I'm doing just fine. "There's nothing to take from you valley and so you're seen as nothing so we toss our scraps and trash down onto you." But mountain man it destroys the homes and ripples holes in our sunny skies, why don't you care? "Those who strive to do and be nothing shall be treated as such valley, learn the laws of life."

Valarie

I have people and animals who care, the most beautiful flowers and vegetation you'll ever see! Water and moist airs, what more could you ask for? I love where I am.

Ever Bright

Scarlet embers burn ever bright and never tires, forever shall burn bright, bright like the night on a starry night ever bright. Bountiful, beautiful brown eyes gaze upon the skies, in awe at the size of the prize ever bright. By sight, beauty in the eye of the beholder, ever bright.

Darkness is heartless but dauntless is the light even in spite of malicious darkness ever bright. Brighter than the divine shine of the sun rise luminescent ever bright. The scarlet blows through the wind never to condescend ever bright. As bright as the armor of the knight hopeful's shining reflection ever bright.

In the end ever bright is the light that shines in the day or the night. Flowing in the wind never to give in to the cold such a sight to behold ever bright. A might yet bold and filled with glee shines bright, ever bright to heights unseen.

Natural Disaster

As shade creeps in, a faint warmth envelopes me, why do I find solace in the dark? Listening to the rain pitter patter the clouds can only hold so much accumulation until they give in, will no one help them carry the load? A straining pain and an insurmountable burden, the dark clouds fill the sky. Rain creates and destroys and destroys its creations, the nature of all things living in its purest form.

Entomb

A chrysalis and a vault which can only unlock from the inside, I reside with the key. Countless colorful butterflies parade within the cascades, I wish I could be one. Will they find my colors undesirable? I'd love to flaunt my wings but I'm scared. Killing myself slowly, the longer I stay here the more I lose the potential me and confide more in the confidentiality of the crypt chrysalis. To emerge is to accept reality and to stay is to decay an easy choice right?

Cease

When one door closes another opens, a life full of opportunities but not for me. My doors revolve, one way in and two ways out and for every minute I'm stuck here the doors I see destined for me close, never again to be. Will I move forward? I can only spin so much until I vomit all hope.

Projects

Over the years broken tears and hidden fears have haunted my dears. They tell their peers and they seem to sneer like they don't care, I try to hear but broken ears deaf to their fears. They sit and cry, I sit and sigh, they try to find a way to hide how they feel inside. By burdens side their feelings reside tucked deep inside. We live inside a generation where it's a shame to hide but they can't abide because what awaits on the other side, ridicule that will never subside.

Elevation

The fall, my demise though we connect through death; the only thing we have in common. As my appendages trickle to the floor like tree, like leaves. The soul. Different colors yet so alike all fade in harmony. Different shapes and sizes yet all living without the fear of patronizing. One with the breeze as we flow carefree and lax.

Hello?

I TRY AND PROJECT MY VOICE BUT NO ONE HEARS ME, not even an echo. THE ROOM IS FULL, after all, misery loves company. SELF LOATHING MISERY'S ESTATE, but I'm alone because it resides in my mind. MINDFUL of the emptiness within. AM I REALLY ALONE? Surrounded by darkness it shrouds the worst. No one can hear me IF IT'S ALL IN MY HEAD.

Existence

A severed pathway caused by the pathogens you emit, even the yellow brick road couldn't save my fantasy. Dismiss my feelings with ease and disease my mind. It's important to feel too. Natural strength opposes the rugged sandbags piled upon my back; I have a hunch you need help too, allow me. Turbulence disturbed my flights from soaring heights. You lance my wings and stomp my hope into the curb. As dusk falls as does everything I yearned to be, the end is nigh.

Life is not a constant, rather death; long live the inevitable. The vultures lurk awaiting my last breath but what defines death when death is undefined? What encompasses the vultures when they pass? A cryptic demise. If everything dies then what's the point in living? What if my purpose is to die, how would I know? I've lived my whole life being circled by vultures leeching my life away, death is all I've ever known so how do I live if everything around me is dead? Except the vultures but why do they want me? My consciousness is straining a night terror that restarts everytime I open my eyes, life.

Label: Maniac

The bleak horizon of the canvas none other than splotches of crimson dissipates my willpower. As an eclipse overcomes me the fog thickens further obscuring my self-worth a vision I see no more. Insatiable shadows devour my demeanor as my mind suffers from mania. What's real is real and what's fake is real, the difference I could never tell, the real danger behind this reality or maybe I made it up.

Dusk

Wipe the dirt and dust off of you, it may anger the clouds. The clouds offer rain for you to be cleanly and pure like them; anything other than that is a stain. If you do not do what the clouds demand of you, they may strike you down with no remorse or repercussion for they are high and we are grime waiting to be purged. The clouds go away at night because they don't like the dark unless they are enraged and unleash a storm but never during the bright white light times. The sky, even higher than the clouds, produces turbulent winds that relay information on where we hide; even when the clouds aren't there, the sky remains so we are never safe.

Nocturnal

No glow in my eyes as the snow drifts and brushes along my skin as there's nothing to stick to. Flakes attempt to reflect the sun's glimmer into me, a frivolous task. I'm not cold because I can't feel, in dark as in light absence is mutual. The frigid winds make my skin pale, who's that breathing down my neck? They're cold, too cold. I'm merely a husk anyway. Hollowed out by scavengers also hollow, an endless cycle as they all feast off of each other never to fulfill their hunger. Dusk approaches, diurnal beings retreat, here I am

Delicate

Half and Half beautiful yet daunting.
A delicate flower the nightshade you devour.
Her nectar a bloody crimson and still, sweet honey awaits those worthy.
She builds colonies, breaks mountains, flourishes nature, annihilates predators, she is love personified.
Nightshade surrounded by a raging inferno proceed if you dare and proceed with caution. She awaits you.

Eternal

My universe, your eyes twinkle and spark, how you light a flame in my soul. Alas the bright light burning, freezes to a halt and the candle fades away. Serenity breeds evil thoughts.

Do I know you?

I'm ok. Ok in a sense that my life somewhat matters but who matters in a world where everyone does, doesn't, and dies. The beginning is trivial as well as the end so what defines what and who matters? Ok in reference to overconfidence in one's significance. What makes you mean more than me? Your accomplishments? Notoriety? Embellishments? When you are forgotten just as forgotten as I, why does it matter? As a matter of fact being forgotten is a matter of not mattering in memory and I'm ok with that

I am

An open canvas so color me as you please, no matter what my values remain. White, black, blue, green, don't label me for your obscenity strikes true. As true as your false pretenses chip away at your own foundation. A sound sensation is to live free as me and be a spectacle to see.

Beware

Approach with caution for the bellowing within the winds sings danger. Serenade yourself among the wicked and release your skinsuit, a wolf in sheep's clothing. Retreat behind the confines of the limited mind, fear has made itself a welcome stay. Fear not the fear itself, fear not fearing what there isn't to fear, a dubious facade, a wolf in sheep's clothing. The sheep in wolf's fur reeking havoc among the wolves, no wonder the wolves target the sheep. The sheep in wolf's fur

Happy

Seek not in the horizon for the radiance to enlighten you. The light in you is radiant enough to illuminate a million others. Nothing more needs to be said. Shine you wondrous star.

Wary of being

Indulge with me in a final dance as the moonlight illuminates our path. Destined to be together as it's written in the stars, they align to show us the way. Low and slow we tread lightly through the soft tones of the lights; particular not to diminish the faint glow. Stay here with me forever my love as we fade into the cosmos.

International means

Conquer not me for all I seek is to exist as I am. Disrupt my peace with your false pretenses of what you own, what you own is arbitrary for at some point you were owned. The hypocrisy of conquering is a void of the past. I am me and everything I claim to be and you are you and every way unique to you so stay in your lane. Harming my way of life is unnecessary, are you not trying to live also? Focus not on me but your own community, begging, crying, screaming to not send their kids to their deaths. Morally obscene knowing one day they won't be objectively seen if this persists. Let me exist. I beg from one person to another, united within a world you too must understand.

You're my glowing bright light in the dimming dark night. The vast sight from our twilight encumbers the night and no low glow to show our love, behold the sun! We together forever in harmony with each other's flaws appall everything to witness it. I love you with all my soul and the visual of your beautiful smile is all I ever need in life to succeed. To hear "I love you" in my ear, oh how I Revere your angelic voice. My one and only choice is to be by your side and confide in you during the dark times in time for the vast sight of our twilight. We stretch the horizon my love.

Buried

A glaring disparity diminishes any hope we had in ourselves. You dare condescend us after all we've done for you? Undermining every word, feeling, thought, action and breath we take. What makes me deserve it less? Clawing my way out of the gutter through dust, dirt, grime, and the bones of my peers; I made it. This hill that they've fabricated for me I will die on and leave a crown behind to notify everyone that no great one made it great alone and everything great beyond that maintains a steady foundation.

Yourself

Lonely days cause my mental state to fade, hiding under the shade, my will to be. But I present society's expectations even when I'm really not okay. So I tread this path hindered by a thread attempting to loosen my balance with gravity. I stomp my feet to the ground and consolidate with the earth as it strengthens my souls. You will not take me.

Death Bed

Indignation stems from the indictment of the innocent. Barred by chains the roots delve into the dark soil and corrupt the once fertile plot. Sprout from under and through the asphalt, show your strength. Refuse to not exist and exist as one for all, for what you provide is invaluable. Everything about you deserves a life and to live it without the regret of regret is in itself a bliss. So be, because you choose to be and blossom; a pedestal is waiting for you. Rise up.

1. Look is all it took
2. Souls bound by a goal
3. Dates to call it fate
4. Eyes scream desire
5. In the frame all thrive
6. years in the making no longer fear
7. words to profess our love
8. years ago we were alone
9. times out of
10. Taking a risk is a risk worth taking.

Scry

Mistake not my silence for absence, I am always here. Close your eyes and heed my cry and understand that it's okay for it to rain. As each drop rushes past your eyes, scry through the reflections and create what you want. Don't fall into the puddle as it may crack your vision. Step by step is the way to tread the path. Every path you choose withholds its own reflection until eventually the rain fades and the sun's rays enlighten you.

Wisps

"Do better" the voices say, as I attempt to fulfill their destiny I lose track of what was meant for me. The pieces don't align with the puzzle so why do I continue? "The will of the wisps never lies." Is all I hear

Father Nature

It's dark yet I can hear the grass inviting me to sink further. Implanting a vision of a beautiful world into my mind I can almost reach it from here but where am I? It's quiet, almost like I can hear the grass not from my ears but as if we're one. Connected with all of nature I listen and seek out their cries for help but what can one person do? They speak of burning, freezing, starving and fighting for their lives, what gives us the right to cause this suffering? If you listen really closely, did you know you could hear nature screaming for help?

Perception v. Intention

Let's talk about perception. Perception is a way of regarding, interpreting, or understanding something; a mental impression if you will. If I say something that o ends you and you perceive it in a negative connotation, whose fault is that? Does the blame fall on both parties? What if how you perceived it isn't how I meant it? This is how perception and Intention clash. Something can be perceived one way but does that rule out the intentions? Think about what you say before you speak. One word could change the course of the world based on how the intentions are perceived.

My Knight in self-deprecating armor

Cast in plated armor I hold this shell to protect me from myself. If I reveal myself, what would you think? Would you hurt me? This armor is my only way to find a place in this world. I can't see myself but who cares, all I care about is how you see me afterall. The sun reflects off and blinds you so you can't see me how I want anyway. Do I take it off so you can see me? Or do I remain within my prison. Protected from harm and judgment but never seeing the world for what it is, is this truly the life I want to lead? One piece at a time I will be released. Look into my eyes. "You're beautiful, thank you for existing"

Be with me.

What is to be? To be as in to exist? To be as in to form? To be as in to be is my definition but what is to be? To be is to live in the present, to live in the now that build the later and avoid what was. After all we are called living beings for a reason, we are in the growing scene and what's growing is the ever expanding life that is now. Thank you for going along this journey with me and I hope you learned a new lesson on the way. This book is my all and there's more to come.

INHALE

EXHALE

MENTIONS

**THANK YOU TO EVERYONE WHO SUPPORTED ME ALONG
THE WAY AND I LOVE YOU ALL**

Gloria	Julian
Percy Sr.	Ashley
Elijah	The Jones Family
Grandma	Uncle Dwight
Nay Nay	Adonis
Lamar	Ms. Tasha
Q diddy	Sara
Bj	Eileen
Savonn	Jack
Gabby	Mickey M
Marvin	Cody Josh S. Park Jerah
Lyric	Kyrah Josh H.
Carolina	Chris H. Jalyn
Alexa Sam	Tia Amber James
Sebastian	Tifani
Yuliana	The Cade Family
Jorge	The Ayala Family
Valdo	The Melendez family

**I apologize in advance for anyone that I left out, thank you and I love
and appreciate you all**

9 798888 107027